T[HE R]EAL STORY

TAI-YISHA JOHNSON

Copyright © Rad Press Publishing
Tai-yisha Johnson

T[he R]eal Story

All rights reserved. No part of this publication may be reproduced, distributed or conveyed without the permission of the author or publisher.

In loving memory to those who lost me
&
to those who made me become stronger

TAI-YISHA JOHNSON

Special thanks to Tennyson.A

INTERLUDE

It's just crazy how two people can mean the entire world to each other and one of them just leave without an explanation or a sense of feeling anything.

It hurt.

I'm hurt.

It'll hurt.

But I had to recognize my strengths and who I was as a woman, before this person entered my life.
Understand that I have dreams and goals that I want to reach before giving my all again to someone.
Understand the concept of self-love and self-care.
Be concerned for my needs for once.
Achieve the things that are going to make me become the woman I want to be in the future.
Inspire those who have gone through similar experience and let them know that pain is temporary.
Wake up with positivity.
When you put out positivity it will return back to you.
Love yourself before anyone.

I was hurting.

TAI-YISHA JOHNSON

DANGERO[US]

T[HE R]EAL STORY

COMBUSTION

Misguided and misused
Fighting with my mind and my heart is leaving me confused
Cause I held it down even through the long nights and long fights Even all alone and you were nowhere in sight
The things that were said and actions that were shown
Are the reasons I gave everything that you should own
But somehow the switch flicked and down everything burned
Up you went and left without showing a sign of being concerned At the end of it all it was you to blame
Cause you painted a picture you weren't able to frame

GUARD

Guarded walls, guarded hearts, guarded emotions
Three things that at least should be open
Hiding to avoid the pain
Hiding cause there's nothing left to maintain
Lies right after the next
Making everything have a negative effect
This leaves no room for comfortability
Which is why we have no stability

T[HE R]EAL STORY

LOVE FADES

My whole heart remains for you
Even when you make it clear that you're through
Everything that I believed in was once there before
But thanks to you leaving now it's all numb and sore

TAI-YISHA JOHNSON

Tired of being tired

T[HE R]EAL STORY

IN? OUT?

One foot in, one foot out
Is it real, I have my doubts
Saying I'm the only one
But showing me that you can always run
How do I know if this is a forever thing
When you're making it feel like we have no string
Guess that's why they say always prepare for the end
Seems so real at times but can also be pretend

TAI-YISHA JOHNSON

OUR LOVE

They say roses are red and violets are blue
You had me so convinced that I was the one for you
So we moved in together had us a little ol' crib
Who would have ever expected everything you said to be a fib

T[HE R]EAL STORY

These are the bridges you burned

LOVE?

I love you
The three words I heard way too soon
But couldn't comprehend the feeling
So I didn't return the words back to you

I love you
The three words I never understood
Until being committed to someone longer than I would
And once that kicked in
It was something I felt internally and knew I was convinced

I love you
The three words that I know and love to feel towards only you
The problem is you left and ran with no trail or even a clue
Left me with confusion and unanswered questions
And when I try to reach out to find it I feel stranded

You love me
You claim to love me, heck even being in love with me
Had conversations about marriage and even a little one to be But because we had some set backs and mishaps you left me to be To figure out what could have went wrong and if it was even me

T[HE R]EAL STORY

VOID

After the six months that it's been I thought I was ready to let somebody in
Fill the void I was missing and replace it with all the touching and kissing
Silly me letting lustful actions contradict how I feel
Without realizing the consequences that would soon reveal
Emotions creep up and it'll create a messy situation
Making the relationship end in a complication
Knowing I should say something to get a clear state of mind
But right now he's the closest thing for me to leave everything behind
Forget about the past
And make the moment last
Just knowing I'll wake up tomorrow wishing I could reset
And not having to feel like this was all a big regret

PLAY

This was the best story ever told
For many including myself it was something hard to unfold
See you were the main character but a terrible actor
Made me believe I was the only star factor
"Once upon a times" and "happily ever afters"
Only left the audience to cry in laughter
Cause I didn't notice when the curtains opened
But the crowd surely knew the moment you roped in
Going through ever scene to know how the ending may be
Just to realize there was really never a you and me

T[HE R]EAL STORY

S Z N

Spring, summer, fall and winter
Four seasons but one became bitter
Raindrop, sunshine, morning breeze till the sun fall
This was something I never noticed at all
One day you got to sleep and everything is clear and bright
The next thing you know you wake up and you've lost sight
Twelve weeks is all it took for the weather to change
The same time frame when you began to act strange
Wasn't sure what was up but I couldn't smell the flowers
Which meant spring and summer were no longer ours
Only hope left was the autumn leaves or the cold white flakes At the end it didn't matter cause both seasons you acted fake You weren't able to communicate how you feel
Which is why our relationship was never real
Spring, summer, fall, winter
I guess all four seasons were really bitter

JANUARY 22ND 2017

The day we met
Is now looking like a regret
Not at first
Although it turned out to be worse
It started as simple as could be
I loved you
You loved me
A couple months later
Things became bitter
The screen of us turned black
And neither one of us knew how to act
The days continued to get colder
After awhile we no longer had the need to lean on each other's shoulder
Slowly we barely even spoke
And I wished that all of this was a joke
Cause that day I knew I should have never caved in
When you wanted the story of us to begin

T[HE R]EAL STORY

If you have to choose between me and her, pick her

ORIGINAL

Similar is what I thought
But there were different actions that he brought
Unfamiliar ways
With the unique things he would say
Convincing me that I was a special one
First place like a gold trophy that he won
Worshiping the ground my feet stepped upon
Then nine months later he was gone
Up and vanished like we never existed
Reason for why the relationship was never persistent
The presumption of thinking he was different
Causes the conflict of whether what we had was significant
Knowing the right things to say to make me believe
That you'd stay forever and never leave
A clown disguised and hidden behind a figure
That I thought was different but is now looking familiar

T[HE R]EAL STORY

UNCONDITIONAL LOVE

The love we built we made through our foundation
Something we created with unlimited limitations
What we had was strong, even hard for some to grasp
But because we were a team we were able to make it last

ONE SIDED LOVE

You left me then came back
And acted like there was nothing in between that
The months you left without a trace
Then coming back asking for some space

T[HE R]EAL STORY

PROMISE TO YOU

There will be a time reconcile
That you miss everything about me and you'll smile
But then realize I'm not there
And no longer will appear
Hit my phone one day and the number ain't the same
Sliding into my DM's trying to spit some flame
Forgetting that a year ago you did me wrong
It took me sometime but I'm finally strong
Not naive so I'm saying I'm done
You keep going thinking this is fun
Just a shame it took you so long to see what you lost
I hope now you know that all your mistakes came with a cost

RETURN

They always come running back
Realizing that you were right and their better half
A reflection of two
Looked in the mirror and always saw the perception of you
But there is only so much one person can take
All this taking some space and us having these breaks
What's the point of leaving to do whatever
The after thought of you coming back when you were doing whoever
The thing is this time when you decided to return
I wont be here but just someone you'll yearn

T[HE R]EAL STORY

A.M

4 a.m and my thoughts begin to linger
As my hair is being caressed with his fingers
What am I doing?
Why am I here?
Letting myself become vulnerable
Is leading me to be miserable
This temporary fix of the need to be wanted
Is consciously leaving me haunted

TAI-YISHA JOHNSON

Our relationship shouldn't be a part-time job

T[HE R]EAL STORY

TRICKS

Illusions
Confusions
Playing mind games
Is leading us to flames
You said I was the queen of hearts
And you were the king of spades
Two different types of art
But you continue to play charades
Continue to treat us like one of your acts
Isn't as cute and friendly as pulling a bunny out of a hat
Its more like tearing us apart
And cutting us in half
Similar to what you did to my heart
But all you wanted was the laughs
To put on a good show for each and every crowd
Is allowing me to do more than to think out loud
With you everything is hidden until you pull it out your
sleeve Which is why I can no longer stay and have to leave

SECRETS

No matter how long the climb
Thing will appear over time
Some for good and some for bad
Certain things continue to add
You think you covered up your tracks
But I already knew and heard the facts
Hiding things not knowing it would show
A couple years later everything decided to blow
You with her
And you with me
You thought you were so sure
That I wouldn't see
You played us both
Even after the wedding vows and our sacred oath
But I share the blame and though it's true sadly
For the last few years I haven't been much happy

T[HE R]EAL STORY

SWING AND MISS

They'll get in your head and make you believe things
Tell you so much and show you what the world brings
You'll believe it and think they're saying the truth
But all they wanna do is hit and swing like babe Ruth
For them this is all a game
Nine innings later you realize that he was just the same
No different from the others in the past
All these strikes knowing its not going to last
Lying to my face not knowing that you left traces
Running from me to her is like your trying to steal different bases
I've caught the ball too many times
That after the third one I've already seen all the signs
There's nothing left and I have no more doubt
But you know how it goes, three strikes and now you're out

Wasted time

T[HE R]EAL STORY

OCTOBER 7TH

You didn't look the same as you once did before
An unfamiliar face I no longer adore
You came back and acted like you never left
The two months gone had created the biggest test
Whether if I can handle not being with you
Took a couple months but I made it through
You were the best thing I did have and that was true
Until the day you decided to leave again, and for that I was done with you

THREE THINGS

Blood, sweat and tears, but mostly tears
The many years of having these affairs
It started off with you
Then ended with me
And finished with us
They say two wrongs don't make a right
The constant lying ending in endless fights
I gave it my all
You gave it your none
Watching it all fall
The mistakes that you've done
Whats more to left to give than to call it quits
Cause you took what we had and crumbled it into bits

T[HE R]EAL STORY

You were incapable of loving me

MARCH 7TH

The feeling of meeting someone new
After the six months of us being through
An intelligent mindset with so much to give
Allows me to be able to finally forgive
That you weren't enough for me
Just a couple things you were unable to fully achieve
I just wanted to say thank you for not being what I need
Because now I've blossomed to a flower just from you planting that seed

T[HE R]EAL STORY

RE-RUN

Going in circles is leading to end up in the same spot
Pretending nothing happened and act like we all forgot
That you left and continue to come back
Thinking I'll be okay with it and not react
Stay for awhile then leave me in the dust
And expect me to lay out my hands and give you all my trust
But this isn't a track field and I wont be waiting at the finish line To congratulate you and to see if you're even mine

TAI-YISHA JOHNSON

Realize his lies

T[HE R]EAL STORY

12 MONTHS

January, February, March
A couple things were said that were kinda harsh
April, May, June
The flowers between us no longer bloom
July, August, September
All the good memories we had I can't even remember
October, November, December
A waste of 12 months of us being together

RE-DIAL

I call but you never answer
Avoiding and dodging the next chapter
Unanswered questions
With false representation of your intentions
You say theres no effort
Even after the four-page written letter
So I decided to give you another call
But still you weren't there to answer at all
To me this is another episode
Call everyday just to get dial toned
I told you what it was from the day you met me
That I'd never give up on us and there'll always be a "we"
But you had a different set of blueprints
Which didn't include me so an "us" no longer exists

T[HE R]EAL STORY

THE BLAME

One night stands
A couple thrown hands
Misused and abused
Always left to be accused
It was always her fault
Or at least that's what she thought
Left and hurt with bruises
Even after all the constant struggle of refusing
No answers to why this is happening to her
By the end of the night her vision is blurred
She tries to leave but always returns
Even after the broken bones and oven burns
She thinks they're in love
Not understanding the repercussion that he has caused
It's sad she thinks that she's the one to blame
When he puts his hands on her and isn't even ashamed

Can't fully forgive nor can I forget

INSECURE

Concerned about your appearance
Fixing certain things to bring up your spirit
Not knowing you looked beautiful from the beginning
That crooked smile that shines when you're grinning
Maybe it's not your looks and something more within
Concentrating on others when you should focus on what you can bring Stop worrying about others and why they're complaining Just know you're a work of art a picture that Gods been painting

OBLIVIOUS

Couldn't see what was right there in your face
Reasoning why you keep asking for some space
Always wanted more and never satisfied with what you had
Gave you all I could and still I couldn't understand
Taking the risk to lose a real good thing Just to have these one night stands and reconnect with your old flings
Not knowing that when the fun is over and you're ready to settle down That the girl that's been pushed to the side will no longer be around Now you get to blame yourself for not caring and being unaware That a perfect women once in your possession is gone, which you can't compare

T[HE R]EAL STORY

Constant Drinking

LIMITED

I cared enough
But you made it rough with all the giving up
Made me think that this thing with us would last
Went through a phase of excitement and now you're ready to blast
Act like it didn't hit you
In the way it hit me
So fast to call it quits and be through
The minute you thought you found someone better and new
I continued to fight
Even when I knew it was no longer right
Gave you my every inch
After the countless nights of having to flinch
You gave me nothing but let downs and distrust
Still to say my heart broke enough for the both of us

T[HE R]EAL STORY

Sometimes love isn't enough to
keep the other person to stay

NO HAPPY ENDING

I wanted the fairytale with the happy ending
The prince saves the princess and lives without pretending
A house that so big I can see our kids running around
Then at night it's just us and we stare at each other without making a sound
A love that's so deep and strong, a bond that can't be broken But then five seconds later there's a bang and that's when I'm woken
You on the couch and me laying on the bed
Something I thought was real was just all in my head
For a second I forgot what you had done
Took our marriage and flipped it by not just having me but another one Living two different lives but always end up back in mine
Then try to talk me down like I'm going to forgive and we'll be fine
That's the thing with fairy-tales and make believe
It'll cloud up your judgment and leave you to be naive

T[HE R]EAL STORY

PRIDE

You let it get in the way of us
I felt it more but to you it was just lust
You said we're just having fun and all you wanted was to fuck But I saw more from your eyes but I guess its just my luck Afraid to show a side that would make you look different
A feeling that's undesirable and even magnificent
There are times you're able to let your guard down
Which allows you to open up and let your feelings for me drown But then it clicks again and your ego steps in Reassuring you that this isn't what you want and that I'm only your friend
If you keep putting your pride before yourself
You'll just get the hand that you've always dealt

Love or Lust

T[HE R]EAL STORY

[ABORT]ION

It's there then in two seconds it can be gone
Something that created two but can vanish in the brisk of dawn Barely met but the connection was real
The minute it was gone my body was unable to heal
Something so beautiful and fragile that's gone in a snap
I knew the love was there or that's what I thought perhaps
All alone and dealing with this on my own
Should have figured you were just another dog chasing a bone Cause when things got hard and complicated you where nowhere to be shown
Unable to find you and your location was always unknown
I dealt with the after math disaster
You were the middle man, the greatest actor
Almost gave life to something that was greater than both of us Something I knew I couldn't handle and with you I couldn't even trust
Brining someone in this world while you're tearing me apart
That day you didn't break just one but two of our hearts

GAME OVER

No matter what system the rules are still the same
Three lives till it's over but for you it's just a game
Keep playing around thinking in the end that you'll win
Not thinking about the consequences thats happening already within
First life gone cause you keep messing around with your ex
Not understanding your fault when there's zero respect
Two lives left not knowing which path to continue on
Is this the part of the game where our love is tested upon
Isn't hard to see that you chose the wrong path to cross
Making me wonder if it's really me whose getting a loss
Next life gone and I can see where I stand
One more to go to see where we are going to land
Last life and the cycle is repeating like a triangle
Not knowing that the controller won't fix what you got tangled Cause you continue to press and click all the wrong buttons Same way you did to my heart and my life then act like you care all of a sudden
You've used all your lives in the same way that you use me

T[HE R]EAL STORY

I want all of you or none of you

BLINDED

Trapped and condoned by this thing called love
Surrounded by the purple rain and the white fluffy doves
Looked at you and all I saw was life
But couldn't see the backstabbing and you holding the knife
I only saw the image of what you could have been
The time we fell in love oh how it makes me grin
Cause you were something, everything that I ever wanted
Something for once in my life that was continuously solid
They say love can be blind but this isn't a movie
Even though you opened up my eyes to show me my own beauty
Those close to me showed me your scams and tricks
The reason this relationship is sinking like ships
I took off my glasses to finally see
The games you've been playing with not one or two but three

T[HE R]EAL STORY

CLOSURE

Was never given the answer for your reaction
Tried to get a hold of you but couldn't receive your attention
Left me with the unknowns
A number with no phone
A location but not your home
Said goodbye I'm on my own
Not knowing the causes
Left me with these broken promises
Struggled for months to get over you
You were head over heels and the only one I knew
But the minute you started feeling confused
Is the moment my heart became too bruised
What bothered me the most was you didn't provide closure
No proper way to know that what we had was over
Opened my messages, no reply, just a cold shoulder
That's why on nights like this I don't remain sober

TAI-YISHA JOHNSON

Suffering

T[HE R]EAL STORY

WALK OF SHAME

7 a.m and I'm unaware of where I am
Bottles on the table and my panty hanging from the lamp
Can't remember the night before
Intoxicated and my vision still blurred
Sneak out before he notices I'm gone
Don't even remember how my night went so wrong
Pictures in my phone with the memory unknown
Went out with my friends but ended up alone
So here comes the part of forgettable nights
All that I know is what's left on my device
Scared to know what happened beyond the frame
Walking out the door feeling ashamed

BODY

More than just a piece of ass
Something worth more and to be labeled with some class
A temple made from above
That deserves more than some smacks but someone to love
Too small or too big
A body size that society decides
The image of what's acceptable
Or something that remains tolerable
The want to fix just to be needed
These are the things that are implemented by the media

T[HE R]EAL STORY

Nothing lasts forever

STRETCH

Gave you a hand but you wanted my whole arm
Always searching for more which is why we're at harm
Couldn't be grateful with the plate right in front of you
Wanting so much you started to lose the main view
The vision of us
Is now something to discuss
Forgetting our promises
The want of you needing to be dominant
Not treating us as one solid unit
But building blocks mingle up on a cubic
Gave you everything that you ever needed
All it did was lead me to catching you cheating
With everything you did I let it stretch
But eventually all the mess just pushed me to the edge

T[HE R]EAL STORY

HAPPY WITHOUT

Smiling and living your life
Like a couple months ago you didn't want me as your wife
Seeing a different side of you now
Made me wonder for all of these years how
Hiding yourself and the way that you are
I thought I seen all the scars and the secrets in the jar
Guess the parts you've shared was at least true
But there were many unknown things that I never knew
Many lies that just opened up my eyes
After all these late nights with these deadly cries
You were no good to me although I couldn't see
Cause I loved you more than anything when all along I should have been loving me

HAPPY

To see you smile gives me some joy
Able to see you happy and are no longer destroyed
Even though you aren't officially mine
I know in due time I'll eventually be fine

T[HE R]EAL STORY

N[EX]T

Gave you all of my years
All it did was leave me with tears
Cause with you I opened up again
A perception of myself, an identical best-friend
Thats the thing when two people become alike
They rub off of each other, simply align
You became my right hand
Somebody I could stand
Could call you my next of kin
Thats how much I was able to let you in
But you continuously wanted to play games
You had a girl with not only beauty but brains
Hope you know the causes of your personal effects
Which is why you're only known now as my previous ex

TAI-YISHA JOHNSON

I am not an after thought

T[HE R]EAL STORY

5 WHOLE DAYS

Yelling, bickering, nobody is listening
The need of wanting to be right is soliciting
Telling me I'm wrong and something else is missing
Not hearing what you want so here comes the hitting
Here comes the abuse, the screaming, and the beatings
The fuck all this shit I'm done, no more I'm finally leaving
Walk out the door takes five steps and starts breathing
Then turns around comes back in and continues the screaming Morning to night with no breaks in between
We both keep arguing and there's no room to agree
Almost a week of miserable mistreats
Just to wake up one day with everything at peace
Took five days for you to understand that my answer wouldn't change Continued on with our life until again you started acting strange Brought it back up again and the cycle is starting to repeat Now I see that you and me are never going to succeed

CONNECTION FAILED

It was real, the both of us intertwined as two
Like cable cords instead we didn't know what to do
Love that was so strong we couldn't see without
The other was like a deserted dessert suffering in a drought
You made me who I was and for that I was proud
Cause now I can see that I can live without
Someone like you who only left me in doubt
Who slowed down my life and made me take a different rout
Had many things going for myself, a future that was bright
And at first you were there to keep me on sight
Our signal and bars were once the strongest
Till that day you left me, alone in August
Thats when things started feeling faded
A phone call away but you were moving jaded
One point we had a full connection
A love filled with endless affection
Now every time I call, no answer, all you got is piled up mail
This just proved that our connection has failed

T[HE R]EAL STORY

IT BEGINS WITH ME

I gave in to you
I dropped and let go of everything for you
I made my world cave in just to surround you
I stayed home instead of hanging with the crew
I gave you all of me
I gave you everything just so you could succeed
I sacrificed my happiness to be able to see you cheese
I wanted for you what I never had for me
I wanted a chance to prove that I was in it for we
I did so much to make sure that the world would see
I knew that at the end I was meant to be with you
I thought that one day we'd finally make it through
I did it all and that's the problem we both can agree
I did everything for you and nothing for me

TAI-YISHA JOHNSON

Emptiness with nothing to fill the void

T[HE R]EAL STORY

IN THE DARK

Things ended bad, all these unanswered questions
Made up things on my own that only led me to depression
Led me straight to finger point the blame
Not on you but something I decided to claim
Cause you seemed perfect no wrong can be done
Even after all the nights that you were gone
You said I was the reason you weren't home and always hid
I believed it but couldn't figure out what I ever did
Made it even worse when you didn't want to share
Figuring things out on my own and being unaware
Left me to suffer now that you already made your mark
Guess you didn't get that everything you did left me in the dark

Stranded

T[HE R]EAL STORY

We crashed and burned
Let me rephrase
You made us crash and I got burned

OUTRO

My love for you was stronger than most
It's still strong even without you here
The love of my life who disappeared
But despite it all ...

I still love you

T[HE R]EAL STORY

[HEAL]THY

INTERLUDE

By loving you, I was losing me
Lost sight of something that was greater than we
Had to figure out what was better for myself
After all the pain that my heart had just felt

T[HE R]EAL STORY

Recovery Mode

TAI-YISHA JOHNSON

On my pursuit of happiness

SELF CARE

Focusing on me, not worrying about you
After everything that happened its time for me to push through
Take care of what's needed
Start from the beginning, re-seeded
Get to understand myself as a whole
All three, mind, body and soul
Take sometime to heal
Concentrate deeply on the emotions that I feel
Figure out how to overcome the hurt
Scratch everything that happened, hit the button re-start
Focus on the recovery of my health
With that take in a fresh life of wealth
Self care is the remedy to start all over
Especially when the relationship ends with no closure

I now know it was never love
Cause love should never cause this much pain
Or even consist of
You to betray and leave me in vain

SELF LOVE

Start to finish
It's time to replenish
People always say love yourself or no one will
I planted that in my brain and screwed it with a drill
My own well-being and sense of happiness
Is at the end of the day going to turn me into a champion
Love who I am with my flaws and all
Even if it takes some time it'll soon all overcome
The things I dislike is what makes me unique
Embrace it all and let it boost my self-esteem
Stop listening to the perception of what others see
Let them know I'll never love someone again more than I love me

SELFISH

Everything I once did for you, I now do for me
Less stressing about where you been and looking at where I can be What brings me joy and the needs to succeed
Rather than crying at night over what is no longer about we
Focused on the better part of me that I lost trying to figure out you And realized that over the last couple of months
I can see that I grew Grew from making people happy and smile over how I feel Have to do it for myself in order to heal
Concentrate on my goals and the future ahead
Tired of people holding me back leaving scars where I bled
For once in my life I'm going to do this for me
Be selfish in order to follow my dreams

T[HE R]EAL STORY

Breathe in, Breathe out

Blossom like the flower you're suppose to be

T[HE R]EAL STORY

BABY STEPS

Half a year later
I've recovered, not fully but greater
Saw all the things I lost in the making
A couple relationships that were breaking
Lost myself and a few things on the way
Took a different route and made it day by day
One foot in front of the other
A day at a time to recover
There's no rush in the process to heal
Just as long as you're trusting the process and accepting the deal That one day you'll reach the moment of redemption Focus everything around yourself with zero exceptions At the end of it all you have to understand That the first step is allowing the heart to hurt from where it began

SELF LEARN

Had to teach myself the things greater than what I would
read How to get over heartache and be able to finally
breathe Learn certain things only one can teach
After that its self taught things that one can begin to preach

T[HE R]EAL STORY

Don't let no man undermine you

FREE

Spread my wings and flew on my own
Thought I was grown so I left my nest at home
Played house for a while till you decided to leave
Then up I left with a chest full of grief
The weight of it was too heavy and I needed to be free
So I replaced the idea of there ever being a you and me
And filled it with the idea of how my life can be
Free from the misery and from what I no longer wanted to see
Rebuilt the image of how I wanna be seen
Saw the vision and turned myself into a queen
Claimed my throne and followed my own rules
No time for these distractions and little fools

T[HE R]EAL STORY

Roses are red
Violets are blue
I am no longer mad
But glad that we're through

JANUARY 22ND 2018

A year since the day we first met
It took a hit but I would no longer say a regret
I learned so much about the mistakes that took place
All that turned out to keep me in a positive grace
No room for hate or negative vibes
I'm over the secrets and all the behind the door lies
I can say without you here I found a place to be content
To put all my joy into something that's more constant
Found my happiness in just working on me
The person I am wouldn't have grown if you didn't leave
So I write this to thank you cause now I can see
That after this date, I'm finally seeing me

T[HE R]EAL STORY

Happiness in solitude

Smile because you deserve to
Shine it bright like he never hurt you

T[HE R]EAL STORY

Growth

POSITIVITY

Wake up every morning with a clear state of mind
No inch in my body wants to feel and be unkind
No harsh words or an urge to even fight
So I wake up making everyday bright
Sunny days only no clouds above my head
No more of those nights of the tears I would shed
More of the days where I cry out instead
From all of the laughter but not by being upset
No room for negative energy
only positive vibes
Stopped stressing about the worries of yesterday
Only forward in the direction where the sun guides

HAPPY

Aspiration
Communication
One without the other
Is like spring without the summer
Or us without some trust
Is the reason I had to adjust
Find my sense of purpose
Keep my head above the surface
To seek more than just a smile
Or a couple laughs that last awhile
But more of something to keep me going
Something constant that keeps on showing
A grin forever lasting
A lifetime of this passion
A clear mind, optimistic
But knowing to be realistic
To live in the mindset of being blissful
And for within to always remain peaceful

I use to smile to hide the pain
But I'm no longer the same
Cause now I have so much to gain
And a crown that I need to reclaim

T[HE R]EAL STORY

LOVED

I still love you but I love me more
Which means there's no room for my heart to continue to be sore
No room for these broken wounds
Or viewed as the girl who once acted a fool
I am now a girl who finally made it through
A woman in control whose ready to bloom
Into something nobody has seen before
A familiar face with a new story to be told
Intellectually creative that many adore
With new tricks and secrets soon to unfold
Concentrate now on the things that reflect positive on me
Not worrying about the opinions of others and what they think
they see
All of this came the minute I knew
That loving myself was better then choosing you

Road to recovery

T[HE R]EAL STORY

Fix your crown girl it's slipping

HIGH MAINTENANCE

Demanding
Not understanding
That there's a difference between the two
Something to this day you still don't have a clue
About how things are suppose to work
Is it cause you no longer felt that spark
Which is why now you want to give it up
Wasted my time and deciding to call in for a sub
Blaming it on me for needing too much
Not realizing that you weren't ever doing enough
I'm sorry you thought I was being pushy
Cause my emotions for you were at the top fully
I'm sorry attention was something that I needed
But I'll never apologize for the way I should be treated

T[HE R]EAL STORY

FOUND

I lost myself in you
But was found because of you
Because the minute you said we were through
Was a realization of the main view
Of how it was meant to be
The new image and perception of me
Who no longer cares about what you do
Or about these little girls that you continue to screw
But concentrates on the foundation
A life filled with unlimited limitations
Endless possibilities
With my many creative abilities
To put everything I have to work
That creates a clear positive outlook
Of who I am as a person
A new and improved version

CURED

Cured from the lies
Cured from the pain
Finally saw the disguise
Superman to Louis lane
No more to hide
But plenty to gain
I no longer cry
Stopped using my heart
But only my brain

T[HE R]EAL STORY

If they don't see your worth
Then they're not worth your time
It's been with you since birth
Just know you're a dime

TAI-YISHA JOHNSON

If you made it this far
To this exact page in this book
Just remember you're a star
Let them all continue to look

T[HE R]EAL STORY

PARADISE

Sunny days and the deep blue sea
No cloud insight just a warm cool breeze
With a colorful view
And some things that I never knew
Kids playing in the distance
Knowing one day my kids will make a difference
Thinking of all the endless possibilities
While living life in only positivity
Over the past drama
That caused my life to end in trauma
I lived and learned
Which pushed me more to getting what I earned
A life that's filled with happiness
With a clear path of success and no patchiness
Knowing that one day I'll eventually love again the right way
And things will work and we wont be pushed astray

TAI-YISHA JOHNSON

I found paradise beyond you

T[HE R]EAL STORY

To be happy is in one's mind
Self control on how you choose to feel

ALONE...BUT NOT REALLY

The beauty of being one
Without the stress and concern of what you've done
Moved on to focus on myself
With things that'll leave me to excel
Putting myself first to make me my one and only
They say to be alone doesn't mean you're lonely
It's a chance to start over
And get to know yourself much closer
Understand who you are as an individual
Know that theres no one like you, you're an original
Sometimes being just with yourself
Lets you know what deserves a farewell

T[HE R]EAL STORY

Once you've healed
Once you've noticed you're ready to move forward
That's when the defense can go down and you can drop the shield
And begin to move onward

LOVE...AGAIN?

Is it wrong?
Should it happen again?
Am I finally strong?
To give this love thing another chance
A little scared knowing how it can end
But with all the growth I can comprehend
Whether someone actually wants to create a we
Instead of making it feel like you're belittling me

T[HE R]EAL STORY

Once you've grown
Into a person who's recovered
You're now someone you've known
That's finally discovered

TWO RIGHTS

They say two wrongs don't make a right
But the two wrongs you did made me write
And although it took me some time to cope
I'm able to write this to give women some hope
Remember that you're stronger than how it may look
And that it all began with the first step that you took
Finding yourself in order to heal
The two things that made everything feel real
Doing what you need in order to succeed
Even if it takes sometime for you to be able to see
That everything has a timing and place
But do everything with a positive grace
Good will eventually comes back to you
Especially with all of the struggles that you've been through
Just thank God for where you are today
Cause the two rights he did was to no longer stay

T[HE R]EAL STORY

Save yourself first

Take some time for yourself
Read it again and try to understand

Y
O
U
R

S
E
L
F

T[HE R]EAL STORY

To all the broken women
Who blame themselves for how others act
You just have to remember that you shouldn't
Be responsible for how others let themselves unpack

You are the definition of beautiful
You are the example of being powerful

T[HE R]EAL STORY

BLISSFUL

Take a moment
Do you hear that?
No more commotion
Only a distant chit chat
No more yelling
Only laughs
Finally smiling
In all of my photographs
This is how it feels
When you finally feel the chills
Less stress
More rest
Nothing is more blissful
Than to operate peaceful

UNLEASHED

I found myself being controlled
No hold over myself but did what I was told
I couldn't see it until I broke free
Someone that was handcuffed just couldn't see
The inability of seeing what was in front of me
My girl pointed it out, it just wasn't meant to be
Although it hurt I knew it was true
The months of us being together was way overdue
Finally got released
But that's what I thought at least
Night of the memories haunting
The constant time of us bonding
All of this forced me to switch
Turn my feelings into something more rich
The power of redirecting energy that's good
Doing more for myself then you could

T[HE R]EAL STORY

Happiness in myself
While you go destroy someone else

TAI-YISHA JOHNSON

It's the greatest feeling of all
To actually feel a sense of being happy

T[HE R]EAL STORY

Roses are red
Violets are blue
No more tears are shed
Now that I'm finally through

TAI-YISHA JOHNSON

Making a commitment with myself

T[HE R]EAL STORY

HAPPY FOR YOU

No matter what you do
No matter where you end
Because of what we went through
I'll be proud because you were once a friend
No more hate
No more anger
I want you to be great
A lifetime of happiness forever
And even though we no longer speak
I hope you're still smiling cheek to cheek
This isn't a sad confession
More of a replenish of my progression
Now that my heart has healed and my mind is healthy
I just wish for everything to go correctly
Pursuing forward
Not looking in the past
Graduate with honors
And make every moment last

I will always love you...

T[HE R]EAL STORY

...but now I need to love me more

Us women need to start empowering one another
Only way to survive in a world of heartless brothers

NEW BEGINNINGS

On the start of a new journey
Alone but the weather is no longer stormy
No longer in the mist
And appreciating life as an everyday gift
Without those around me
And supporting the route of my recovery
I wouldn't turn out how I wanted to be
About to crack a smile that turned out so lovely
I thank the lord everyday
Allowing my setbacks to turn into comebacks
Wiping the windows that are no longer grey
Allowing nothing bad to get in the way

TAI-YISHA JOHNSON

It must hurt in order for you to feel better

T[HE R]EAL STORY

It hurts less
But I'd be lying to say that it no longer does
I can say that I'm now feeling bless
And no longer have hate in my heart

The secret to healing
Is that there's no secret at all
You have to come to terms with all your feelings
In order to rise when you fall

T[HE R]EAL STORY

It's possible to let you go and still love you
But I will no longer hurt from you

TAI-YISHA JOHNSON

Everything that occurred
It happened for a reason
You have to grow from the experience
No matter how long the season

T[HE R]EAL STORY

He hurt you, yes
But don't ever give him the power of thinking he got the best of you
You're stronger than anything in this world
Never give up your hopes and dreams

To heal
To truly heal
And to be in a position where you feel normal
Will take time

Everyone heals at their own speed...

...for me it took almost a year

T[HE R]EAL STORY

Looking and reflecting on the past
does help you move forward

TAI-YISHA JOHNSON

Everything's lovely

T[HE R]EAL STORY

Many will ask what's the secret of healing
There isn't one
And one's answer isn't defined for everyone
You have to find something or a way to understand your feelings
With this then begins the progress
Of how to accept what has happened
And realize that moving on is the best remedy
Harder to do than just simply saying it
Just begin taking things slow
Deleting photos, messages, anything that would make you feel
low
Once these distractions are gone
Then the process of healing can be acted upon
Healing in the sense of taking care of one's self
Self love, self care and knowing your self worth
Once these are achieved
You'll begin to feel a new you
You're perspective on life and people will change
Living life in more of a positive setting

10/7

This exact date I'll never forget
Mostly because now I wish we never met
You never understood, and still can't till this day
The months that you left and then you made me pay
Blaming me for the strain on us
But never did look at yourself not even once
You made what we had dangerous
Doubted the trust that we had in us
I didn't get it because one day we were good and the next we weren't
Like leaving the stove on, looked away for a second and everything got burnt
You wanted your break and I tried to give you that
But things didn't add up with you then you called it quits behind
my back
Never made sense, you left with no respect
Making me look at everything with a regret
At the end you said you were no longer happy
I told you I respected that but deep inside it affected me badly
Left with no closure
Trying to find the missing pieces within the folder
Searching so much that it's only hurting me in the end
In need to fix my heart and let the pain begin to mend
This is when I realized I needed to let my soul heal
Let my inner self discover something that's more real

T[HE R]EAL STORY

Replace the hurt I was feeling with a positive learning
Become a better me, a healthier person
Learn the core values of self worth and love
Understand that you deserve everything, all the above
The minute you get right with yourself
Is the minute you can give the negative a farewell
Remember in any situation to put yourself first
To love again takes time and shouldn't be forced
I've grown spiritually and mentally from the hurt
I symbolize the rose that grew from the dirt

OUTRO

This is the end
At least for this chapter
A story told by a few
But many tend to listen
Pain is a temporary substance
But can turn out to be a blessing
I've recognized my weaknesses
And overcame them with my strengths

I feel happy

I feel happier

I can finally say...

...I've finally moved on

ART COVER / OVERVIEW

The art cover is to symbolize the message that the overall book is representing. As simple as it may be with a rose growing from it's roots and risen within the hand, this concept is to indicate growth and within the growth becoming a healthier person in the perspective of one's self and the outlook of life in a positive manner.

The art cover was created by Ahniel Lee, also known as Povrich and book was edited by Mohamed Jawal.

TAI-YISHA JOHNSON

Thank you

www.ingramcontent.com/pod-product-compliance
Lightning Source LLC
Chambersburg PA
CBHW032042290426
44110CB00012B/919